W9-BFV-572

BLACK BEARS

Jack Ballard

FALCONGUIDES

GUILFORD, CONNECTICUT
HELENA, MONTANA

AN IMPRINT OF GLOBE PEQUOT PRESS

Copyright © 2013 Morris Book Publishing, LLC

FalconGuides is an imprint of Globe Pequot Press.
Falcon, FalconGuides, and Outfit Your Mind are registered trademarks of Morris Book Publishing, LLC.

Photos by Jack Ballard unless noted otherwise.

Project editor: Staci Zacharski
Text design: Sheryl P. Kober
Layout: Sue Murray

Library of Congress Cataloging-in-Publication Data

Ballard, Jack (Jack Clayton).
  Black bears / Jack Ballard.
    pages cm — (A Falcon pocket guide)
  ISBN 978-0-7627-8493-6
  1. Black bear. I. Title.
  QL737.C27B3477 2013
  599.78'5—dc23

                          2013024234

Printed in the United States of America

10 9 8 7 6 5 4 3 2 1

To good friends and trail mates:
Bill Powell, Chris Madson, Kevin and Andrea Rhoades,
and most of all, Lisa.

Contents

Contents

Acknowledgments

State wildlife agencies across the country have compiled and published comprehensive information and research regarding black bears. It is largely due to their efforts that bears are thriving and this acknowledgment is a public "thank you." Special thanks to Dr. Chris Servheen, Professor of Wildlife Biology at the University of Montana and Grizzly Bear Recovery Coordinator for the U.S. Fish and Wildlife Service, for reviewing and making helpful comments on the manuscript.

Introduction

The neighborhood was astir. Telephones rang, engines turned, and kids scrambled from their houses toward the vehicles. In less time than it takes to summon a take-out pizza, a cavalcade motored down the dusty gravel road, intent on entertainment, Montana-style.

The occasion was not a party or something as sensational as a shooting. A black bear sow and two cubs had wandered into the foothills ranching community of my childhood. When approached by a neighbor's pickup truck, the bruins scrambled up a towering cottonwood tree overshadowing an abandoned homestead.

A youth of 6 or 7 years, I peered eagerly out the window as we turned from the county road toward the sagging cabin and a gathering group of onlookers. High in the branches, partially obscured by the tree's waxy green leaves, I spied a large black form and two smaller ones. The sow was easier to see, but my gaze focused more acutely on the cubs. They were fuzzy and cute. One had a small patch of white on its chest.

A decade would pass before I sighted another black bear, this one high in the Bridger Mountains. Hiking with two brothers and friends, we paused to rest on a rocky outcropping above a clearing that we'd just passed through. A glance down our back trail set my senses on alert. An immense, coal-black bear with a shining coat came lumbering out of pines and into the meadow. Even to my untrained eye the bear was huge. Visions of snarling bears on the covers of sporting magazines plagued my imagination. Suddenly the entire hiking party was aflame with energy. We covered the next mile in record time.

Three decades later, black bear sightings have become a more common part of my outdoor experience. As I write this, I can see a band of open slopes dotted with aspen trees along the eastern face of the Beartooth Mountains. Should I train my spotting scope on the mountainside, I might spot a black bear, for I've seen them there in my ramblings. Like most other regions of the country, the number of *Ursus americanus* occupying Montana has risen substantially in the past few decades.

Years of observation and study have changed the vision of black bears I held as a youth. Those open-mouthed bruins on the magazine covers, I've come to realize, were trained grizzlies and black bears that a handler induced to snarl while a photographer snapped a photo. With black bears in particular, these portrayals do not reflect reality. They are normally shy beasts and rarely aggressive; animals deserving our respect, not fear.

As black bear numbers in North America continue to rise and their range expands, more and more people will have the opportunity to observe them firsthand. I offer this book in hopes it will help the reader better understand and appreciate these intriguing creatures.

CHAPTER 1

Names and Faces

Names and Visual Description

The "black bear" is the name given to the most widespread and common species of bear in North America. However, this name is somewhat misleading. Not all black bears are black. In the northwestern United States, a significant percentage of black bears are brownish or reddish-brown in color. "Cinnamon bear" is a term sometimes used to describe black bears with coats exhibiting brownish or reddish hues. Elsewhere, black bears may sport coats intermixed with black and lighter hairs, giving them a bluish appearance. Black bears in some areas may also rarely be

Black bears were named for their coat color as most commonly seen in the eastern United States, but not all black bears are black. Shutterstock

cream-colored, or have small to quite large patches of white hair on their chests. The black bear's scientific name, *Ursus americanus,* is derived from *ursus,* the Latin word for "bear" and *americanus,* a term that refers to the species' home continent. In some respects, adopting the English version of the black bear's scientific name as "American bear" might help dispel notions about the animal's color based on its common name.

However, if you consider the origin of the species' moniker, it's easy to understand why they became known as black bears. When Europeans began colonizing North America, their first explorations and settlements were in the eastern part of the country. At that time, black bears were abundant in the eastern forests. Black bears in the eastern United States are normally black in color and rarely exhibit the variable hues noted above. Thus, the term "black bear" was very appropriate for the species as encountered by colonists in the east.

Compared to more streamlined predators such as wolves, foxes, mountain lions, and bobcats, black bears appear bulky and slow, although they are deceptively fast and agile.

Viewed from the side, black bears have a large, rounded rump. The highest part of the rump on a black bear may be taller than the point of its front shoulders. Like other bears, the skull of the black bear is broad but tapers quickly in the region of its eyes to a narrow jaw and nose. The side profile of a black bear's face is straight or slightly convex (rounded outward). Animals with darker coats sometimes have tan hair on their snouts that contrasts with their black noses. Bears with black coats may also display small patches of tannish hair on the forehead near the eyes.

Black bears have fairly large claws that, unlike the claws of a cat, cannot be retracted into their toes. The claws of a black bear are often visible at close range, but may not be readily observed at a distance. A very short, stubby tail is found on the rump, but has no readily known purpose.

The taste and texture of bear meat has been historically likened to that of pork. Perhaps that is why male black bears are known

The claws of a black bear are dark and curved. They're much easier to see at close range.

as "boars" and females are called "sows." Baby black bears are referred to as "cubs."

Related Species in North America

Black bears share the North American continent with two other species of bears: polar bears and grizzly bears. Polar bears, *Ursus maritimus,* are creatures of the far north, ranging across the frozen regions of Alaska, Canada, and the Arctic islands. In Alaska, the range of black bears does not extend as far north as the polar bear's habitat. Polar bears are white or nearly white in color, and much larger on average than black bears, making it unlikely that any competent observer could confuse the two species.

Polar bears are also much different than black bears in their foraging habits and diet. While black bears are omnivorous, eating grass, nuts, insects, berries, eggs, and nearly anything else that has nutritional value, polar bears are carnivores. The diet of the great bears of the north consists primarily of seal. Polar bears have longer necks than black bears so that they can more efficiently thrust their heads into holes in the ice to capture seals.

The grizzly bear, *Ursus arctos,* is the black bear's other relative in North America. Black bears inhabit much of the same range as the grizzly, making it probable the two species might be encountered in proximity in the northern Rocky Mountains of the contiguous United States, over much of Alaska, and in numerous areas of Canada. Because black bears and grizzly bears share many characteristics, biologists often remind recreationists and wildlife watchers to avoid using any single characteristic to distinguish between the two species. Instead, laypeople are advised to focus on several identifying features to determine if an animal is a black bear or a grizzly bear.

Color variations may be helpful in some situations, but color is not a reliable way to tell the two species apart. A bear that is uniformly jet-black in color is probably a black bear. However, grizzly bears can have coats that are a dark, dullish brown color, making them appear black in certain lighting

Black bears share the North American continent with two other bears: the grizzly bear and polar bear. SHUTTERSTOCK

conditions. Just because a bear is blonde or brown doesn't make it a grizzly. As noted previously, black bears may have coats that are similarly colored.

Adult grizzly bears are substantially larger on average than adult black bears. However, many full-grown black bears are just as big as immature grizzly bears. Where their ranges overlap, big black bear males may be as large as smaller grizzly bear females. Thus, although a 600-pound bear is almost undoubtedly a grizzly, variations of mass in the two species in relation to age and gender make it very difficult to separate the two North American bears based upon size.

Beyond color and size, several other traits can be analyzed to distinguish a black bear from a grizzly. First of all, in contrast to the straight or convex profile of the black bear's head, the head

Although similar in size to a black bear, the dished face, prominent hump, short ears, and grizzled appearance identify this young bear as a grizzly.

of a grizzly looks slightly concave or dished. Additionally, a grizzly bear's claws are very long, light-colored, and readily observable compared to the shorter, dark claws of a black bear. Grizzly bears usually exhibit a noticeable hump on their front shoulders, which is absent in black bears. However, depending on the posture of the bear, grizzlies may appear to lack the shoulder hump and a black bear's shoulder my seem humped. In most cases, the ears of a black bear appear longer in relation to its head and body than those of a grizzly, although the season and the length of an animal's coat may confound such an evaluation.

Although voracious consumers of nuts, berries, and other plant matter, grizzly bears are more likely to consume large prey than black bears. Grizzlies don't often target healthy animals in their predation attempts, but will readily kill weak or injured animals as large as caribou, elk, or moose, and are capable of bringing down much bigger animals than all but the largest black bears.

Subspecies

Biological literature commonly reports sixteen different subspecies of black bears in North America. However, many contemporary bear experts question whether there is enough genetic, behavioral, or morphological variation among the historically identified subspecies to warrant such classification. In some cases, subspecies were identified on the basis of dominant hair color. Other subspecies were designated in relation to populations of black bears inhabiting certain regions that might have slightly different physical characteristics, such as bigger teeth or larger average body size, than bears observed in other areas. However, the extent to which such variation is caused by local factors, such as nutrition, versus distinct genetic lineage is not well known. Some research on black bears suggests that at least in terms of genetics, just a few subspecies inhabit the continent, certainly not sixteen.

Interestingly, the confusion surrounding how to classify bears with different sizes and color schemes from various parts of the continent is not a recent problem. On May 31, 1806, while camped with the Nez Perce in Idaho, Lewis and Clark appealed to the natives to help them distinguish a number of bear hides they had accumulated. The Nez Perce separated the "Hoh-host" (grizzly bear) hides from the skins of the "Yack-kah" (black bear). They went on to explain to members of the expedition that grizzly bears have long claws and are much more ferocious than black bears. Separately in their journals, though apparently after consultation, Lewis and Clark concluded that the predominantly black-haired black bears they encountered along the Pacific Coast were the same species as the black bear or "common bear" that they were familiar with in the eastern part of the country. They believed that the reddish or cinnamon-colored black bears they encountered in the interior Rocky Mountains of Idaho and Montana were a separate species, distinct from both grizzly bears and the black-colored bears found along the Pacific and Atlantic Coasts.

Lewis and Clark mistakenly identified the brown and reddish black bears of the central Rocky Mountains as a distinct species from black or grizzly bears. SHUTTERSTOCK

Rather than catalog sixteen debatable subspecies, it seems more helpful to point out trends in coat colors among black bears and highlight several unique populations. A comprehensive study identifying the location and coloration of more than 40,000 black bears in the United States and Canada revealed several definite trends. In the eastern United States and Canada, the vast majority of black bears are black, with other color phases increasing as one moves westward toward the Great Lakes region. In western Ontario and Minnesota, approximately 5 to 10 percent of black bears exhibit non-black coloration. Black bears in the northern Rocky Mountain regions of Montana, Idaho, and Wyoming show the greatest diversity in color. More than 80 percent of individuals in local populations may have coat colors other than black. Biologists in Washington's North Cascades National Park found that of 1,586 bears observed, more than 30 percent had fur that ranged from nearly white to dark brown. In the Rockies, the percentage of bears with black coats increases from north to south and from east to west. Many more bears living in the mountains near the Pacific Coast and in the southern Rockies have black coats.

Although variations in coat color are a fascinating element of black bear biology, they generally play a minor role in sub-species identification. However, one subspecies of black bear, the Kermode bear or spirit bear *(Ursus americanus kermodei),* contains individuals that display a very unique coloration. Kermode bears inhabit dense rain forests along the British Columbian coast and nearby islands. The term "spirit bear" stems from the fact that a percentage of these black bears are colored exactly the opposite—they are white, but not albinos. The white fur represents a genetic mutation similar to that found in red-haired humans. A recessive trait, white-furred bears occur when two adults (who may both be black) transfer the recessive gene to their offspring. Where the Kermode bears range on the mainland of British Columbia, only about 1 to 2.5 percent of the bears are white. That percent-age increases dramatically on some of the islands inhabited by these unique black bears. On Gribbell Island, one of many islands located near the mainland, white-colored bears represent some 30 percent of the population.

Other subspecies of the black bear are not identified on the basis of such dramatic physical features as the Kermode bear. Instead, they're usually distinguished by geographic isolation from other populations of black bears. The Mexican black bear *(Ursus americanus eremicus)* is found only in western Texas and northern Mexico. It is currently listed as a threatened species by the state of Texas. Potential bear habitat also exists on the eastern side of Texas, which may one day be occupied by the Louisiana black bear *(Ursus americanus luteolus),* which is presently found in Louisiana and southern Mississippi. Not far to the east, the Florida black bear *(Ursus americanus floridanus)* ranges across Florida, southern Georgia, and portions of Ala-

The Louisiana black bear is listed as a threatened species under the Endangered Species Act. USFWS/GARY STOLZ

bama. Many Florida black bears display a patch of white hair on their chests. Both the Louisiana and Florida black bear subspecies are currently listed as threatened under the Endangered Species Act. Their status as subspecies is due to their geographic isolation and limited habitat. The extent to which their genetic makeup differs from northern populations of black bears has not been extensively researched.

In Alaska, the Haida Gwaii black bear or Queen Charlotte black bear *(Ursus americanus carlottae)* is a subspecies found on the Haida Gwaii or Queen Charlotte Islands near the coastline of British Columbia. These bears tend to have notably large skulls and molars. Genetic studies of the Haida Gwaii bears have attempted to determine the extent to which this subspecies might have been isolated from other black bear populations during prehistoric periods of glaciation. At least one of these studies provides some evidence of a coastal lineage of black bears in western North America that differs from bears found on the mainland.

Will the widely publicized designation of sixteen subspecies of black bears persist in the future? Intense study and genetic analysis of creatures such as the grizzly bear and gray wolf have sharply reduced the number of subspecies in relation to those theorized in earlier times. It is likely that further genetic research and biological study of the black bear will reduce the sixteen to less than a half-dozen.

Physical Characteristics

Black bears show a remarkable variation in size. Due to differences in available nutrition and the energy bears must use to obtain it, black bears in one part of the continent might be considerably bigger or smaller than those found elsewhere. Within specific populations, however, mature males are notable heavier than females on average. Research studies in Idaho and Pennsylvania have found males to be nearly twice as large as females. Some of the size variation between the sexes is due to maturational patterns. While females normally obtain maximum weight by the time they are 4 years old, males may continue to grow to age 8 or beyond. A New York study of black bears revealed that the average 3-year-old male weighed as much or more than the typical 8-year-old female. In addition to its greater weight, the skull of a black bear boar is about 10 percent larger than the head of a female of similar age.

The weight of a black bear may fluctuate by 30 percent or more depending on the season. Bears are heaviest just prior to entering hibernation (see Chapter 4) and lightest when they emerge from their dens in the spring. Bears in the eastern part of the contiguous United States tend to be larger than those found in the West. Northern bears obtain weights that are usually a bit higher than those found in more southern climates. However, the

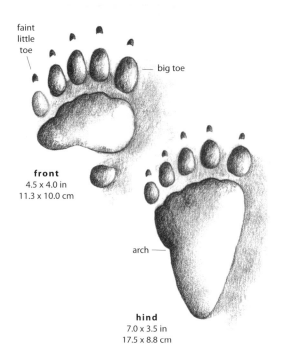

faint little toe

big toe

front
4.5 x 4.0 in
11.3 x 10.0 cm

arch

hind
7.0 x 3.5 in
17.5 x 8.8 cm

Large black bears can achieve weights well in excess of 500 pounds. SHUTTERSTOCK

DOES FUR COLOR MATTER?

The bewildering range of colors found in "black bears" is a phenomenon unequaled in any other indigenous mammal of North America. "Wild" horses display a remarkable range of color, but they are a feral population (domestic animals that have become wild) not native to the North American continent. Grizzly bears range from very dark brown (nearly black) to almost fawn-colored specimens. Gray wolves range from white to gray to coal black. But none of these species contains the variations of black, bluish, white, blonde, reddish, and brown associated with the black bear.

More than mere novelty, scientists theorize that the color differences among black bears have important biological functions. Research has demonstrated that the white Kermode bears are more successful in catching fish than their black counterparts. Biologists believe that salmon are not as frightened of light objects looming above them as dark ones, an attribute favoring the white bears. The most uniformly black populations of black bears are found in dense forests, such as those on the Pacific Coast. Some biologists believe the dark color makes it easier for the bears to blend in with their shadowed surroundings, making them more efficient hunters and less easily spotted by potential predators. In more sparsely treed areas, such as the northern Rocky Mountains and northern California, where many bears are cinnamon- or blonde-colored, it's possible that the lighter variations allow them to dissipate heat more efficiently in the summer.

Like the biological traits that facilitate the survival of other species, the diverse colors of the black bear may be an important adaptation.

tendency of north-dwelling members of a particular species to be larger than their southern counterparts (Bergmann's Rule) is not as pronounced in black bears as many other species, including their grizzly bear cousins. Thus, determining an average weight for the two sexes of black bears that is consistent across the continent is very difficult. Males probably range from around 130 to 550 pounds at mature weight in various parts of the country. Corresponding females reach weights of about 90 to 360 pounds.

How large can black bears grow in the wild? Mammoth specimens have been recorded in a variety of locations. Numerous boars killed by hunters or vehicles in the fall have topped the scales at 800 pounds and beyond. In December 2011, an 829-pound male was shot in New Jersey. An 879-pound boar was taken by a hunter in Pennsylvania in 2010. The same bear weighed

Biologists theorize that the lighter color phases of black bears found in the interior Rocky Mountains may help adapt them to the habitat in which they live. Shutterstock

700 pounds when captured by biologists in New Jersey in June 2009. In 2001, a black bear was struck by a vehicle and killed near Winnipeg, Canada. The huge animal depressed the scale to 856 pounds. Biologists estimated its live weight at nearly 900 pounds.

Like weight, other physical dimensions of black bears are highly variable. The animals range from about 4 feet to 6.5 feet in length from nose to tail. Adult bears may stand from 26 to 42 inches at the front shoulder. The rear paws of a black bear are longer than its front feet and may measure from around 5.5 inches to 9 inches. A black bear's rear paw prints look something like the barefoot track of a human with noticeable claw marks in front of the toes. The bear's front paws are broader and more squarely shaped than the rear.

CHAPTER 2

Range and Habitat

Historic Range

Black bears may occasionally roam across open areas where trees are absent or limited, but are primarily associated with forests. They're equally at home in the deciduous woodlands of eastern North America and in the evergreen timberlands found in the Rocky Mountains and coastal regions of the West. Black bears may also inhabit the more arid scrub forests and shrublands of the

Black bears range across many habitats in North America, but are primarily creatures of the forest. SHUTTERSTOCK

Southwest. But rarely are they year-round residents of regions lacking some type of forest cover.

Prior to European settlement, much more of North America was forested or contained significant patches of timber and shrubland. Exceptions included the far north, in the tundra regions of Alaska and northern Canada. Desert areas in the Southwest, including most of Nevada and portions of California, Arizona, and Utah, were also largely devoid of trees. Significant forested regions were also absent in Baja California and southern Mexico. But otherwise, varying levels of tree cover were present across the continent.

Black bears are found in Alaska as well as the contiguous United States. This bear is standing on the bank of Alaska's Russian River. SHUTTERSTOCK

Destruction of forest habitat for logging and farming was a primary factor for plummeting black bear populations in the 1800s and early 1900s. SHUTTERSTOCK

Highly adaptable and omnivorous, black bears were historically able to survive nearly any place that had timber, making them residents of almost all of North America. Except for the desert Southwest, the bruins inhabited virtually all of what is now the contiguous United States. Their clawed footprints scratched the soil of the entirety of mainland Canada south of the Arctic Circle. They also inhabited essentially all of Alaska except for the arctic regions. Black bears ranged well into the northern reaches of Mexico, primarily in the mountains. The animals were also found on most islands along the Pacific Coast capable of supporting bear populations. Black bears probably colonized various islands by swimming from the mainland or perhaps by crossing ice bridges during periods of glaciation.

Settlement of North America by Europeans occurred rapidly in the 200-year period from the beginning of the 1700s to the early 1900s. Several trends associated with this settlement greatly reduced black bear numbers and range. First of all, bears were actively hunted for their meat, hides, and fat. The fat was rendered into bear grease, which was sometimes used as shortening for cooking, as leather dressing, in cosmetics, and for other purposes.

However, the destruction and elimination of black bear habitat probably exerted more negative pressure on bear numbers than hunting. Logging cleared vast tracts of forest, converting it into treeless farmlands inhospitable to the timber-loving bruins. Black bears, like other predators, were also actively persecuted with traps and poisons ro remove their perceived threat to humans and livestock. On the plains of the Midwest, where black bears were associated with treed areas along major river corridors and other riparian areas, cutting timber for homesteads degraded their habitat and also brought them into association with humans happy to kill them for food or to simply eliminate the possibility that a black bear might dine on a sheep or raid a hen house for eggs. In the contiguous United States, hunting, persecution, and habitat loss extirpated black bears from most of the southern and central portions of the country. They persisted in remote, timbered areas of the Northeast, upper Midwest, and Rocky Mountains, primarily in places unsettled or avoided by humans.

Current Range

Clearing forested lands for timber and agricultural use, along with unregulated hunting, were the primary culprits in black bear decline. Nationwide, black bear numbers probably hit their lowest levels between the 1920s and the 1950s. During this time, however, societal changes slowly occurred that made it possible for bear numbers to increase and populations to reclaim segments of habitat from which they'd been eliminated. Hunting seasons were enacted in most states that protected bears from unregulated and year-round killing. North Carolina, for example, enacted its first bear-hunting season in 1927. Over time, this season became restrictive to maintain bear populations. In 1927 the season spanned two-and-a-half months and had no limit on the number of bears a hunter could kill. In 1947, a yearly bag limit of two bears per hunter was enacted. The limit was reduced to one bear in 1971. Arizona instituted a bear-hunting season in 1927, which converted to year-round hunting throughout much of the 1940s, an era in which agricultural interests believed the only good bear was a dead bear. Restrictive seasons were re-established in 1954, leading to a gradual increase in the state's bear population.

Along with protections from unregulated hunting, black bears began to benefit from changing land use practices during the twentieth century. In the East, in places such as New York's Adirondack Mountains, designation of land as state or national parks protected bears from hunting and preserved their forested habitat. Numerous areas where farmers cleared and attempted to raise crops were abandoned due to soils that were too rocky or infertile to sustain grains or vegetables. Mountainous areas across the country, heavily logged for large, old-growth timber, began the process of reforestation. Fast-growing deciduous trees and shrubs are often the first species to recolonize cleared timberlands, resulting in dense undergrowth that creates fine habitat for black bears and providing them with the fruit, nuts, and berries that make up a large portion of their diet.

Black bears now roam throughout most of their historic range in Canada, except for the expansive farmlands of southern Saskatchewan, Manitoba, and Alberta. In 1937, black bears were extirpated from Prince Edward Island and have not been reestablished. They range across most of the forested regions of Alaska, but are absent on the Seward Peninsula, in the Yukon-Kuskokwim delta, and north of the Brooks Range. They're abundant on many of the islands of southeastern Alaska, but are absent on many of the large islands that are occupied by grizzly bears.

Small populations of black bears are found in the southwestern United States. This bear was photographed in the Sangre de Cristo Mountains in New Mexico. SHUTTERSTOCK

In the contiguous United States, the largest segments of habitat harboring black bears occur in the northern portion of the country and extend along forested mountain ranges to the south. Elsewhere, bears occur in fragmented and isolated pockets of habitat. In the northeast, black bears are abundant in Maine and are found as far south as Virginia and West Virginia. Bears are most abundant in the Appalachian Mountains, where their range extends as far south as the northern border of Georgia. More isolated populations of bears are found along the coastal regions of southern Virginia and North and South Carolina. They also survive in rural, forested tracts in varying numbers in Florida, Georgia, Mississippi, Alabama, Louisiana, and eastern Oklahoma. The Ozark Mountains of Arkansas and southern Missouri represent the largest intact area of currently occupied black bear habitat in the South.

The dense, secluded forests in the Great Lakes region were an important refuge for black bears prior to the enactment of hunting seasons and the era of wildlife conservation. Today, bears are plentiful in the timberlands of the northern reaches of Minnesota, Wisconsin, Michigan, and the entire Upper Peninsula of Michigan. Further west, their primary range is found along the Rocky Mountains from the Canadian border southward through Montana, Idaho, western Oregon, Wyoming, Utah, and Colorado. They also occupy the large expanses of forest in the coastal mountains of western Washington, Oregon, and California. Black bears inhabit the Sierra Nevada mountains of central and north-central California. More isolated, sometimes very small populations are located in various regions of New Mexico, Arizona, and western Texas.

Due to the large ranges they inhabit, reliable estimates of black bear populations in North America are difficult to obtain. Various sources differ substantially in their assessments of how many bears live on the continent. Best estimates indicate some 100,000 to 200,000 black bears inhabit Alaska. The Canadian population includes another 320,000 to 400,000 animals. Approximately 285,000 to 350,000 bears track the forests of the contiguous United States. It is not known for sure how many black bears occupied North America prior to European settlement, but some experts believe the current population is nearly equal to presettlement numbers.

Black Bear Habitat

Black bears are avid consumers of plant matter, much of it from trees and shrubs in the form of fruit, nuts, and berries. Some black bears also find suitable habitat in swamps or desert scrub. The small population inhabiting western Texas is one example of black bears existing among scrub vegetation in an arid climate. Swamp-dwelling black bears occur in the South and boggy areas of the north, including a population in the sprawling Okefenokee Swamp that covers portions of Florida and Georgia.

Depending on the location, the forested habitats with which the black bear is most strongly associated may be quite different. In Arizona, for example, black bears are found among several different types of forest including pinyon-juniper woodland, oak woodland, pine and mixed conifer forest, and chaparral (stands of woody, drought-tolerant, evergreen

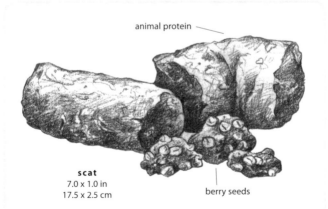

animal protein

scat
7.0 x 1.0 in
17.5 x 2.5 cm

berry seeds

Black bears may inhabit both deciduous and coniferous forests, from rain forests to locations that are quite arid.

shrubs). These habitats contrast markedly with the moist, deciduous forests of the Great Lakes region or the rain forests along the Pacific Coast, where black bears make their homes in very different surroundings.

Bears may exist in many types of woodlands, but the best black bear habitat offers the creatures both a buffer from human habitation and access to a variety of nutritious foods. Bears in northern climates hibernate for extended periods of time during the winter. Hibernation requires the animal to gain substantial fat

Nuts and berries, like these chokecherries, are critical food sources for black bears in many habitats.

reserves in the fall to provide the energy needed to survive winter. Deciduous forests containing trees that produce mast (nuts or berries) represent excellent habitat for black bears. The oils found in acorns that fall from oak trees, for example, allow bears to quickly gain fat reserves when the nut crops become available in autumn. Although oak trees are absent from the northern Rocky Mountains, coniferous forests are often interspersed with fruit-bearing shrubs such as huckleberries, chokecherries, and raspberries. Regions containing berries or other fall-ripening fruits represent superior habitat to forested areas lacking such richly nutritious food sources.

BEARS AND NATIONAL PARKS

The creation of national parks in the United States, beginning with the designation of Yellowstone National Park in 1872, gave refuge to black bears and other large carnivores. National and state parks played an important role in the protection of black bears in the twentieth century and continue to offer undeveloped habitat for these fascinating animals. Across the country, national parks are some of the best places for wildlife enthusiasts to observe black bears.

Bears are typically most visible in the spring, shortly after they emerge from hibernation. They're often spotted in the fall as well, as their feeding activity increases in preparation for hibernation. Black bears are most frequently observed by park visitors in early morning or late evening, the first hour or so after sunrise and before sunset. Here's a list of major national parks known to be inhabited by black bears, the state, and a vigilant observer's odds of seeing a bear on a multiday excursion if he or she visits during the seasons of greatest bear activity.

A black bear prowls the forest in Great Smoky Mountain National Park. National and state parks were very instrumental in the recovery of bear populations. SHUTTERSTOCK

NATIONAL PARK	STATE	SIGHTING ODDS
Acadia	ME	Low
Great Smoky Mountain	NC/TN	High
Shenandoah	VA	Moderate
Yosemite	CA	High
Yellowstone	WY/MT/ID	High
Glacier	MT	High
Everglades	FL	Low
Big Bend	TX	Low
Olympic	WA	High
Crater Lake	OR	Moderate
Grand Teton	WY	Moderate
Rocky Mountain	CO	Low
Denali	AK	Low
North Cascades	WA	Moderate

CHAPTER 3

Forage and Nutritional Requirements

Basic Food Sources and Digestive Biology

Technically classified as carnivores, the strong, stocky bodies of black bears are more suited to overturning rocks, swimming, or tearing apart rotting logs than pursuing prey. Wild canine and feline predators such as wolves, red foxes, mountain lions, and lynx feed almost exclusively on the meat of the prey. Black bears, by contrast, often receive 90 percent of their annual nutrition from plant matter.

Although black bears tend toward a vegetarian diet, their digestive system is not as specialized as that of an elk or whitetail deer when it comes to breaking down plant material. The ungulates have very long digestive tracts in which several compartments with specialized bacteria and functions aid the digestion of plant material. The digestive tract of a black bear is longer than that of a wolf or mountain lion, but shorter than that of ungulates. This makes it possible for bears to gain substantial nutrition from plants, not just meat. But they are unable to capably digest the woody twigs of shrubs and trees, or the mature grasses commonly consumed by hoofed mammals. Thus, black bears are quite picky about the types of vegetation they eat and must ingest large amounts of plant matter to acquire sufficient energy and nutrients.

Because they inhabit such a broad geographic range in North America, and occupy so many different types of woodlands, scrub forests, and swamps, summarizing the diet of black bears is a nearly impossible task. However, it is possible to characterize their food sources in general terms. Certain types of foods are consumed by black bears nearly everywhere they're available, be it Denali National Park in Alaska or Great Smoky Mountain National Park in Tennessee.

Black bears receive most of their nutrition from plant matter. This bear is eating berries and foliage.

When it comes to plants, black bears usually target specific species at the period in the growth cycle when they are most tender and nutritious. Researchers in New York's Adirondack Park have concluded black bears consume more than thirty different types of plants in the park. Succulent shoots of grasses and sedges are eaten by bears. They also relish broad-leafed plants such as alfalfa, clover, and dandelions. Certain parts of plants, such as flowers and roots, are also eaten by black bears. In comparison to grizzly bears, however, whose massive claws and exceedingly powerful forelegs make them very adept at digging, black bears are less likely to expend considerable effort in unearthing roots, bulbs, and tubers. Other ground-growing food items for black bears include mushrooms and the newly emerging heads of some fern species.

In many parts of the country, black bears eat dandelions. SHUTTERSTOCK

Blueberries and rose hips are commonly eaten by black bears. Lisa Densmore blueberries

Low-lying shrubs that produce berries or other edible seeds and nuts are important sources of nutrition for bears in a broad range of habitats. In the Rocky Mountains, in places such as Yellowstone, Grand Teton, and Glacier National Parks, these may include wild raspberries, huckleberries, and rose hips (the fruit from wild rose bushes). In the Adirondacks or other locations in the Northeast, black bears feed on wild cherries, elderberries, blackberries, and other species. Nearly anywhere they're found, black bears have at least some access to fruit produced by low-growing shrubs.

Moving into even taller vegetation, black bears glean nutrition from many different types of trees. They happily consume many varieties of nuts, including the nuts found within the cones of some evergreen trees and deciduous species. Apples, plums, and other fruits, domestic or wild, are highly prized by black bears. Bears may also eat the fuzzy catkins of trees in the poplar family.

Black bears supplement the vegetarian diet with a wide array of other foods. They're large animals, but most of the living things they eat are quite small. Bears are known to eat a surprising range of worms and insects, including earthworms, ants, various grubs, grasshoppers, moths, caterpillars, beetle larvae, and even some species of bees and wasps. Insects are often caught by the black bear's long, sticky tongue. The nests of multiple bird species, from geese and ducks to forest-dwelling grouse, are raided for eggs or to catch newly hatched birds unable to escape. Nests in trees are sometimes raided, but most of the eggs and hatchlings taken by bears are from the clutches of ground-nesting birds. In the swamps of Florida and elsewhere in the deep South, bears may also raid alligator nests, sometimes confronting female alligators when they steal their booty. Black bears may also eat frogs, although their consumption of amphibians and reptiles is rare.

Some species of mammal are also preyed upon by black bears, depending upon the geographic region and habitat in which the bears live. The newborn young of hoofed animals, including mule and whitetail deer, elk, caribou, and moose, are sometimes eaten in significant numbers by black bears. In some locations, roaming bears happen upon the young creatures and kill them opportunistically. Researchers also believe black bears deliberately hunt young ungulates, such as elk calves, in areas where females are known to birth their young year after year. Black bears may also kill adult and subadult individuals, almost invariably targeting the injured or weak. Beavers, ground squirrels, mice, and voles may also be taken by black bears. Infrequently, bears may kill and consume smaller predators (often the young), such as bobcats, wolves, red foxes, and coyotes. Historical records also indicate that adult black bears (typically males) may kill and eat members of their own kind.

Fish is another notable source of nutrition for black bears in some places. Like grizzly bears, many populations of black bear on the Pacific Coast rely upon runs of spawning salmon for food.

Its long, sticky tongue helps the black bear lick up a variety of insects. SHUTTERSTOCK

Black bears are capable fishers. On the Pacific Coast, fish are an important part of the diets of some bears. SHUTTERSTOCK

Inland bears may also learn to catch fish, most often preying on the spawning runs of species that use smaller streams for reproduction, such as trout. Black bears may also ambush other types of fish, especially those found in shallow water where the bruins can easily catch them, including catfish, carp, and suckers. When berry and nut crops are sparse, some biologists have concluded, bears put more effort into fishing.

Forage Preferences by Season

The black bear's diet is perhaps the most flexible of any animal in North America. At any given time of the year, bears may have a dozen or more local food sources available to them. That said, black bears display strong seasonal preferences to various types of food.

In the springtime, black bears emerge from their dens lean and hungry. After enduring months of winter dormancy, it takes their digestive systems a couple of weeks to regain their full function. In most places, the end of hibernation coincides with the beginning of the annual growing season for trees and plants. Springtime forage for black bears thus includes the soft, new shoots of grass and sedges. They also seek broad-leafed plants that sprout early in the season, such as dandelions and skunk cabbage. Budding vegetation on certain trees, including quaking aspen catkins, offers another source of nutrition for bears in the spring.

While black bears are snoozing away in their dens during the winter, the conditions outside may challenge the survival of hoofed animals sharing the bears' habitat. Each winter, old or weakened ungulates such as deer, elk, moose, caribou, and bison succumb to starvation. If the winter is very long or includes extended periods of intense cold and deep, crusted snow, other segments of the ungulate population are also susceptible to winter kill. Deer enduring their first winter are more vulnerable than adult animals. Aggressive males may lose most of their fat reserves during the frenzied activity of the fall breeding season or be recovering from battle wounds, making it more difficult to survive a brutal winter. Tough winters that take a heavy toll on ungulate populations provide a bounty for bears emerging from hibernation. The bruins are able to scavenge the carcasses of winter-killed animals, giving them access to high-protein forage in large packages. Bears in some areas, such as Yellowstone National Park, dig small rodents like pocket gophers from their shallow burrows. They may also snack on insects and worms that become active in the spring, including night crawlers and earthworms.

As spring transitions to summer, bears encounter a broadening food base. Ungulates often birth their young in June. Black bears are able to add newborn deer and the offspring of other hoofed animals to their diet in many regions. Summer-flowering plants are consumed by bears that may eat the

Black bears eat fireweed, a flowering plant that often sprouts after forest fires.

blossoms, stems, and roots. Fireweed, a broad-leafed plant with pinkish-purple flowers, grows abundantly in mountainous areas in the Northwest, especially after forest fires, as its name implies. Black bears eat fireweed and other flowering plants, including spring beauty and glacier lilies, and cow parsnip. Mushrooms may also become part of a bear's summertime diet.

Some black bears gain a surprising amount of nutrition from insects. Since most bugs are active and abundant during the summer, that's when bears are best able to key on them for food. One of the continent's smaller insect species, the ant, is actively hunted by the bears of the Great Lakes region and in other parts of the country. Bears don't normally dig ants from ground-dwelling colonies, but instead seek those living in rotted logs. They tear the logs apart and adeptly eat the insects in the pupal and larval stages of development, along with the worker ants that may be tending them. When berry and nut crops fail in locations such as northern Minnesota, ants become a very important food source for bears. A bear may not put on fat by eating ants, but these high-protein morsels allow them to maintain their body condition in the absence of other foods.

Perhaps the most important source of summertime nutrition for black bears is berries. Raspberries and other early ripening species become available in July in many locations. As the summer progresses, other fruit species mature, allowing bears to move from one berry to the next. The calorie-rich berries help bears develop their fat reserves for the winter. In turn, the seeds of the berries are distributed to new locations in the scat of the berry-munching bears. Researchers have concluded that some Minnesota black bears may eat more than 30,000 berries a year.

Berries and other fruits may persist as food options for bears in the fall. But in many parts of the country, nuts are the preferred menu item for bears wherever they're available. Hazelnuts are relished by bears. Black bears may travel substantial distances, 20 miles or more, to reach habitat niches

This bear has climbed an oak tree, probably in search of nuts. Black bears are voracious consumers of nuts in late summer and fall. SHUTTERSTOCK

THOSE GLORIOUS GUT PILES

Hunting seasons for deer and elk in the contiguous United States, along with moose and caribou in Alaska and Canada, often coincide with the black bear's most active feeding period in the fall. Human hunters usually "gut" or "field dress" the animals they kill, removing the internal organs to avoid meat spoilage and making carcasses easier to transport. In remote locations, hunters may also leave behind the head, hide, and rib cage of an animal they've harvested, as these parts of the carcass are heavy and not eaten by humans.

Black bears (and grizzlies) readily consume the gut piles and other portions of game animal carcasses left behind by hunters. Occasionally, a bear may find the carcass of an animal killed by a hunter but not yet retrieved. The bear may claim the bounty, sometimes resulting in a potentially dangerous human-bear confrontation when the hunter returns. Black bears are generally much less aggressive toward hunters returning to a carcass than grizzlies, but in either case, wildlife officials discourage hunters from attempting to retake a carcass from a protective bear.

While the internal organs of ungulates killed in the fall typically contain high fat reserves that go a long way toward fattening a black bear for its winter hibernation, the windfall may come with a cost. In addition to a potentially fatal confrontation with a hunter, many gut piles contain lead fragments. Bullets used in hunting rifles are most often composed of a lead core with a copper jacket. Upon impact, bullets often fragment, sending small pieces of lead into the meat, bone, and/or internal organs of a game animal.

Researchers have recorded higher than normal blood lead levels (BLLs) in birds (bald eagles and ravens) that scavenge elk carcasses left behind by hunters in the Jackson, Wyoming, area. A local study found an average of 145 lead fragments per gut pile in animals killed by hunters. Some wildlife experts worry that even though bears are much larger than eagles or ravens, requiring more ingested lead to cause serious harm, incidental lead poisoning from scavenged gut piles could be negatively affecting the health of black and grizzly bears in some places.

Fortunately, there's a simple solution. Ammunition composed of copper and other non-lead materials is becoming more popular with hunters. It's just as effective as lead-based bullets, but doesn't pose a risk to bears or other creatures that share a hunter's bounty. With this in mind, an increasing number of hunters are choosing to go "unleaded."

flush with nuts. Sharp claws enable black bears to climb trees in search of nuts, giving them an advantage over ground-bound creatures that also eat mast. The cones of the whitebark pine tree are collected by squirrels in huge caches in the northern Rocky Mountains. Nut-bearing cones of other evergreen species are similarly horded by squirrels elsewhere in the country. Black bears often discover and raid the caches to eat the nuts from the cones. I once observed a black bear in Montana eating pine nuts from a squirrel cache. The enraged rodent would descend down the tree above the cache, chattering fiercely at the robber. It would drop to a branch just inches above the ears of the preoccupied bear. The bruin intermittently raised its head or lifted a paw toward the squirrel, sending it scampering back to the treetop. An amusing incident for the watching human, it wasn't nearly so appreciated by the upset squirrel.

CHAPTER 4 Abilities and Behavior

Physical Abilities

Black bears are large, shaggy animals that may be rolling in fat in autumn. To the untrained eye, they look neither swift nor athletic. However, black bears are surprisingly quick and very strong.

Over short distances, black bears can sprint to about 30 miles per hour, nearly as fast as a fleeing deer or roughly the same pace as a galloping horse. Their dense fur and compact bodies overheat rapidly, limiting the distance over which black bears can fully exert themselves. Nonetheless, they can vanish in a heartbeat when alarmed, or make an effective predatory chase on other mammals when given the opportunity. A black bear can easily outrun the fleetest human. Thus, if confronted by a bear, it is futile to attempt flight. Instead, experts advise people to stand their ground and appear as imposing as possible, a subject we'll explore in chapter 7.

Along with their speed, bears are impressively strong. Researchers have observed young black bears easily overturn large, flat rocks weighing 350 pounds to unearth the insects underneath. While hiking in early summer in western Montana, I once happened upon a hillside where a black bear had been eating insects living under stones. The bear had flipped over a dozen or more rocks, each as large as a coffee table. It had also pried up several boulders that were nearly buried, stones that were about twice the diameter of a basketball. Black bears commonly use their powerful shoulders and forelegs to rip apart fallen logs to expose ants, grubs, and other insects. Their claws are shorter than those of a grizzly bear, but still very effective in demolition when coupled with their stout forelegs and paws.

Black bears are also very strong and efficient swimmers. Although they don't look like Olympians slicing artfully through

Black bears are excellent swimmers and will cross rivers and lakes in search of food.
Lisa Densmore

the water, two physical characteristics help bears swim with ease and a surprising amount of grace. The same strength that powers their forelegs in turning over rocks and ripping logs apart allows them to propel their bulky bodies through water. Black bears are also quite buoyant, meaning they float rather than sink. Air trapped in their dense fur provides the buoyancy, as does body fat, which is less dense and provides more flotation than muscle. While canoeing one summer on a mountain stream in central Montana, I watched a young black bear splashing about in the shallow water at the river's edge, apparently enjoying the cool pool on a hot July afternoon. When it spotted the canoe, it swam effortlessly across the strong current, then scrambled up a towering Douglas fir tree along the bank, dripping enough water from its coat, it appeared, to fill a bathtub. Various sources report that black bears can swim 3 to 5 miles per hour and have been recorded swimming as far as 5 miles. While that distance is certainly exceptional, black bears are extremely comfortable in the water and will readily swim across rivers, to islands along the seacoast, or on freshwater lakes in search of food.

Can bears climb trees? A certain amount of confusion exists regarding this question, and such misconceptions sometimes factor into other erroneous beliefs. Some people think bears are unable to climb trees and that shinnying up the nearest trunk is a potential means of escape in a bear confrontation. While it's true that large grizzly bears are generally unwilling to climb trees, young grizzly bears sometimes do so.

But what about black bears? In fact, black bears are much more adept tree climbers than grizzlies. Young black bears are extremely agile in trees. Faced with danger, black bear cubs (and often their mothers) will scurry up a tree for safety. Large black bears probably use trees less often than smaller bears. Yet even robust adult males may climb a tree to break off branches bearing nuts or fruit, or to investigate a beehive in a hollow tree for honey. The tree-climbing prowess of black bears can be traced to their sharply pointed claws and dexterous paws.

Sharp claws and strong legs make black bears very adept at climbing trees. They may shinny up a tree in search of food or to escape predators.

Their claws can dig firmly into the bark of a tree, while the sophisticated touch of their paws allows them to grasp branches somewhat like a human. Once up a tree, black bears do not turn and descend face first as some creatures do, but "back down" like a person would.

Black bears walk "plantigrade," a scientific way of stating that the entire foot has contact with the ground. Bears share this physiological feature with humans. Plantigrade locomotion allows a creature to maintain superb balance while moving and to traverse challenging terrain with ease. Due to their plantigrade rear feet and unique skeletal structure, black bears can stand on their hind legs for extended periods of time, unlike hoofed animals that can "rear up" on their hind legs but are unable to balance that way for more than a second or two. While moving in search of food, black bears often pause to stand on their hind feet. Biologists speculate the bears assume such a posture to give them a better view of their surroundings and perhaps to aid their sense of smell. In the presence of an unidentified danger, black bears will often stand on their hind feet and actively scan their surroundings to pinpoint the threat. A similar strategy may also be used when a bear detects potential prey.

The sense of smell is often touted as the black bear's most highly developed perceptual ability. In 1991, researchers from the North American Bear Center in Minnesota observed a black bear sow with twin cubs sniffing the air. Her nose led her on a remarkable journey spanning three days and covering 41 miles. Her trek ended in an area with a high density of hazelnut bushes, drooping with a bumper crop of nuts. Five weeks later the family returned to their home range, the mother shepherding two of the heaviest cubs the researchers had ever seen.

Specific tests of the smelling abilities of various animals are difficult to design and perform. However, biologists widely believe that the olfactory sensitivity of bears ranks among the greatest of any mammal in the world. Inside a black bear's nose is a very large nasal cavity enclosing a complex system of mucus membranes.

Black bears can easily raise themselves on their hind legs. Such behavior allows the bears to obtain a better view of things that have caught their attention. SHUTTERSTOCK

The scent-detecting mucus membranes of a black bear is up to 100 times larger than that of a human. Some scientists theorize that a black bear's sensitivity to smell may be 1,000 times greater than that of the average person. Black bears use their exceptional smelling abilities to find food, but scent is also extremely important for detecting animals that might represent a threat, gathering information about other bears in their territory, and bringing boars and sows together for mating.

For decades, folklore pertaining to bears assumed that because their smelling abilities were so developed, their other senses were weak. Black bears are sometimes characterized as having poor vision and hearing. However, researchers have demonstrated that bears have a capacity for hearing and vision equal to or better than humans. One study found that black bears were very capable of discriminating between different colors. Their ability

A Wyoming black bear tests the air. Many experts believe a bear's sense of smell is its most highly developed perceptual ability. Shutterstock

Black bears are sometimes characterized as having poor vision and hearing, but they see and hear as well or better than humans.

to distinguish color and their good close-up vision, along with their uncanny sense of smell, are now believed to be important to their foraging strategies. Observing the color and shape of berries on a bush, for example, may give bears important visual cues concerning their desirability as food items.

Research concerning the hearing abilities of black bears is lacking, but our continent's most numerous bear probably hears as well as humans and may be capable of detecting pitches beyond the range of people. Naturalists and casual wildlife watchers have seen grizzly bears and black bears reacting to noises at ranges well beyond what would be expected of an animal with stunted hearing capability. Of the three species of bears in North America, black bears have the largest ears in relation to their body size. This may indicate that black bears have the most highly developed sense of hearing among the three.

Black bears may appear large and clumsy, but certain parts of their bodies are capable of precise movement. Their claws are attached to large paws, but can be used skillfully to find a crack in a hollow log with an insect colony inside, or to slide under the lid of a closed garbage can to pry it off. The long tongue and front teeth of a black bear are also very sensitive and adept. Bears can lick up ant larvae while ingesting few of the adult insects, or nip individual blackberries from a vine. Despite their bulk, black bears are capable of surprisingly refined tactile skills and also have a superb sense of balance.

Vocal and Visual Communication

Black bears have a wide range of vocal communications and body postures by which they signal their intentions. Along with scent-marking, these are the primary ways by which they communicate with their own kind and give verbal and visual signals that can be interpreted by knowledgeable humans.

The sounds made by black bears are not typically as loud as those commonly emitted by some other creatures, such as a bugling bull elk, a bellowing bison, or a honking flock of Canada geese. However, bears make several types of noises that indicate whether they're content or disturbed. In the den, newborn cubs may make a noise similar to a cat's purring. Cubs most commonly use this sound when they're nursing, but may also emit the motorlike hum when in close proximity to their mother and very content. A loud screaming sound, very similar to the cries of a terrified human child, is associated with a bear cub in distress. In rare instances, female black bears have investigated the sound of a crying child, evidently thinking it was a cub in distress.

Cubs may also seek to attain a sow's attention with a bawling noise, which may indicate they want food or may communicate displeasure with other aspects of their world. Sows respond to the vocalizations of cubs with their own noises, sometimes grunting to gain their offsprings' attention, such as when they want the

Cubs are often more vocal than adult black bears. This frightened youngster has climbed a tree and is bawling for its mother. SHUTTERSTOCK

cubs to descend from a tree. Adult bears may greet one another by clicking their tongues or emitting a high-pitched, friendly grunt. Agitated black bears often blow air forcefully from their lungs in a woofing sound and may clack their teeth together. A frightened bear, such as one cornered by a dominant animal or one that has climbed a tree to avoid danger, may emit a moaning noise, indicating its fear.

Along with vocalizations, black bears communicate their mental states with body language. A bear standing on its hind legs is usually alert and may be looking for something or reacting to a sight or scent it has yet to identify. Upright ears and a fixed gaze also signal alertness. Ears laid flat on the head may indicate submission or potential aggression. Conflict between black bears usually occurs in relation to competition for mates or food. Black bears are normally solitary creatures, most frequently encountering one another during the mating season or at food-rich areas when nutritional resources are concentrated, such as during the spawning run of fish or on a hillside flush with berries. During these encounters, conflict is usually settled in relation to the dominance hierarchy or "pecking order" of bears in the area, with larger bears intimidating smaller ones. However, sows can act abnormally fierce when protecting food resources for themselves and their cubs, sometimes successfully repelling boars twice their size. During these encounters, complex behavioral cues, including foot stomping, jaw popping, and circling may be part of how a bear evaluates the threat posed by a rival.

Hibernation

It's commonly known that black bears hibernate during the winter. But when does hibernation begin, and what happens to bears as they snooze through the long, cold nights of winter in a den?

Preparation for hibernation begins long before a black bear excavates a hole in the earth or crawls into a hollow log for its winter slumber. During late summer and autumn, black bears enter a behavioral phase known as "hyperphagia." In people, hyperphagia is fancy way to say they're overeating and likely to become obese. Hyperphagia describes essentially the same process for black bears, but instead of resulting in an unhealthy condition, becoming fat is absolutely essential. A bear's metabolism slows dramatically during hibernation, but it still needs enough energy to sustain itself through the winter.

In the northernmost portion of their range, black bears may spend up to seven months of the year in hibernation. In the northern portions of the contiguous United States, they commonly pass four to five months in hibernation. Fat reserves gained during the hyperphagia period, during which bears gorge on nuts, berries, and other food sources, are essential to winter survival. Large black bears may add 150 pounds of fat to their frames before denning for the winter. Black bears normally lose 15 to 25 percent of their body weight during hibernation, necessitating a considerable increase in weight before winter. Nursing females may lose even more body mass, sometimes emerging from the den 30 to 40 percent lighter than when hibernation began.

The hibernation of black bears is different than that of other hibernating animals, such as marmots. While the body temperatures of rodents drop drastically during hibernation (sometimes more than 60 degrees F), the temperature reductions in bears are quite modest (5 to 10 degrees F). Rodents also awaken occasionally during hibernation to eat and pass body waste. Bears may go without expelling waste for months. Their urine is recycled and their digestive functions come to a halt. While rodents are incapable of arousing to perform coordinated physical functions during hibernation, bears can "wake up" quite quickly.

Black bears are often portrayed as hibernating in caves, but large underground caverns are not used as dens. Bears instead seek out smaller quarters. They may hibernate in crevices between rock slabs or in holes created by overhanging shelves of stone. More frequently they excavate an abandoned badger hole or coyote den, or simply dig a hole of their own. Black bear dens excavated in soil generally consist of a short shaft, just large

Black bears normally lose 15 to 25 percent of their body weight during hibernation. In the fall they're constantly on the lookout for food. SHUTTERSTOCK

enough to allow the bear's body to pass, ending at a slightly larger "room" with just enough space for the bear to turn its body. Hibernating bears may also use hollow logs as dens, and smaller bruins are fond of dens located in tree cavities located 10 feet or more above the ground. These dens protect the young bears from predation. Both wolf packs and larger bears are known to prey upon denning black bears.

With all the effort it takes to locate or dig a den, it seems bears would return to the same winter resting spot year after year. Such is not the case. Black bears seldom reuse a den, although some dens may be used for years by different bears. I personally observed a den in Montana utilized by various bears over a ten-year period. While it's possible that a few of the dennings were by the same bear, variations in track size indicated multiple animals.

Some bears don't hibernate in a den at all, but make a nest of grass, leaves, or other plant material and sleep above ground. Scientists believe the plant matter in the nest keeps the bear's body above moisture that might collect on the ground. Black bears also sometimes opt for more sophisticated dens. They're known to sleep in crawlspaces under rural cabins, or to slip into the crumbling foundations of abandoned buildings. In western Montana, a sizeable black bear once invaded a lakeside cabin, ransacking the interior. When the owners visited their retreat on

Some people believe that black bears hibernate in caves, but they're more likely to dig a hole or a den under logs. USFWS/Karen Laubenstein

NON-HIBERNATORS?

The duration of a bear's hibernation increases in northern latitudes. Black bears in northern Canada and Alaska usually spend two months longer—or more—in hibernation than bears in the lower 48. The season of hibernation decreases even further as one moves south. Pregnant sows and females with cubs den earlier and become active later in the spring than males. Big boars are the last to enter their dens in the fall and the first to exit them in early spring.

In the deep South, in Florida and Alabama, some black bears may not hibernate at all if food sources are plentiful. Conclusive research has yet to settle the matter, but some biologists believe female black bears in Texas hibernate (at which time their cubs are born), but the males do not. If such is the case, a similar pattern is probably also at work among black bears in Mexico.

Certain physiological characteristics serve important functions in some places, but not in others. Weasels living in northern climates turn white in the winter, while their southern kin remain brown. Hibernation is often viewed as the black bear's most unique adaptation, facilitating its survival. But like the notable adaptations of other animals, its presence may decrease or disappear when it no longer serves a purpose.

New Year's Day, they thought it had been burglarized, but noticed the only thing missing was bedding. Imagine their surprise when they found the bear snoozing amongst their pillows in the crawlspace under the floorboards of the cabin!

While denning, a black bear commonly curls up with its head tucked firmly against its chest. Thermal imaging of the bodies of hibernating black bears shows the greatest heat loss in the area of their eyes, noses, and foreheads. A bear tucking its head against its chest evidently isn't just assuming a cute sleeping posture, but is reducing its heat loss during hibernation.

CHAPTER 5 Reproduction and Young

The Mating Season

Black bears mate in June over much of their range, but the mating season can begin in May and persist into July. Some biologists speculate that preparation for mating begins much earlier. As noted in the previous chapter, large males are the first to emerge from their dens in early spring. Why do they come above ground before springtime plant growth has begun, when there's still very little forage available? It's possible that their early break from hibernation gives them more time to range across large territories and scout for females. In fact, the home range of black bear boars is much larger than sows. In Michigan, the home range of males covers an average of 335 square miles, while females' home range averages 50 square miles. Researchers in Minnesota have concluded the mating range of dominant males can cover 80 to 160 square miles and may encompass the home range of a dozen females. While the home range of a female sometimes overlaps the ranges of other females, dominant males repel other males from their territories during the breeding season.

Although boars commonly reach sexual maturity at age 3, they usually don't have an opportunity to breed in good habitat until much later. Older, larger males prevent them from breeding. Females may reach reproductive capability at age 2, but don't normally breed until age 3. In poor habitat in the far north, where food resources are limited, females may not breed until 6 or 7 years of age.

Black bears are promiscuous, meaning a male may mate with more than one female during the breeding season, and a female may mate with more than one male. Black bears often have twin cubs and triplets, and due to their promiscuous mating habits, the cubs within a single litter may all have different fathers.

Males locate females during the breeding season primarily through their sense of smell. They also announce their own presence

Due to the promiscuous mating habits of black bears, these twin cubs may have different fathers. Shutterstock

within the home range through scent-marking. Boars utilize "bear trees" as signposts. They gouge the trees with their claws, usually reaching as high onto the tree as possible, a behavior that probably gives other bears an indication of their size. They also rub their bodies on the trees and may leave bite marks as well. While boars are highly tuned to the scent of females during the breeding season, their attention is very selective. Females nursing cubs will not breed and are avoided by males, as are females too young to breed.

Pregnancy and Gestation

After breeding in early summer, a female no longer tolerates the company of males. Her focus turns to food—to ingesting

Females that have mated feed heavily during the summer. Their fat reserves must be sufficient to nourish themselves and developing cubs during hibernation. SHUTTERSTOCK

enough forage to sustain her during hibernation and to nurture a litter through pregnancy. Black bears (along with grizzlies and polar bears) are among a number of species that experience delayed implantation. For most animals, an egg attaches to the uterine wall of the female shortly after fertilization and begins fetal development. The process is different for bears. The fertilized egg (or eggs in the case of multiple offspring) experiences a limited amount of development (cell division) but does not attach to the uterine wall. It "floats" in the uterus for the remainder of summer and into the fall. If the sow has gained the necessary fat reserves to nourish herself and maintain a pregnancy during hibernation, the embryo attaches to the uterine wall and gestation begins. If not, the embryo is simply absorbed into the body of the female.

Defining the gestation period (the amount of time between the beginning of pregnancy and birth) is somewhat confusing for bears. Although the female's egg may be fertilized in June, significant embryotic development may not begin until November. Thus, the gestation period could be defined as beginning when the egg is fertilized (in late spring or early summer) or when it attaches to the uterine wall and embryotic development begins (in late fall). Biological reference works typically report the gestation period of the black bear at around 215 days, the time from mating until cubs are born. However, it's important to remember that a considerable portion of this time includes delayed implantation. An embryo's uninterrupted development, from implantation until birth, takes only eight to ten weeks.

Birth

Most large mammals birth their young in the spring or early summer. The birthing period usually occurs just prior to a season when food is plentiful. Canines and felines, such as wolves and mountain lions, birth their young before hibernating rodents emerge and before baby deer and elk are born. This allows the adult predators to nourish their young with easily caught prey.

Hoofed animals birth their young at about the time plants become very green and nutritious in spring, enabling females to produce abundant milk for offspring.

Why then are black bear cubs born in January or February, in the weeks that uncannily coincide with the coldest days of the year? Biologists speculate that birthing very small cubs allows a sow to avoid the nutritional demands of a pregnancy that produces much larger offspring at birth. Newborn black bear cubs are very tiny. Most weigh less than a pound, coming into the world at around eight ounces and 9 inches in length. The average wolf pup is twice as large as the average black bear cub at birth. Although the average adult coyote weighs only thirty pounds, their newborns are nearly identical in size to those of the much larger black bear.

The average litter size for black bears is two cubs, but litters of three or four are not uncommon. SHUTTERSTOCK

Birthing such tiny offspring in January rather than May actually gives young black bears a survival advantage. Like their parents, baby black bears need to gain lots of weight before hibernation. Their mid-winter birthday allows them to be older and larger when they confront their first physically demanding season of hibernation, increasing their odds of survival.

The birth of her cubs occurs around the midpoint of winter dormancy, but the sow is awake during the birthing. Black bear litters range from one to six cubs, but twins are most common. Cubs are born blind and covered with sparse, gray fur. They are immediately cleaned of birthing tissue and fluids by the sow. While this behavior, common to most mammals, is also thought to imprint the scent of her offspring on the mother, the process is probably different for bears. Researchers have found that hibernating sows will readily accept an orphan cub, but once fully awakened in the spring will reject or even kill an unknown cub. This behavior has led some biologists to conclude that even though a sow is alert while birthing her offspring and aware of their movements and needs, her sense of smell may be limited or dormant during hibernation.

The first few weeks of the cubs' lives are spent nursing and snuggling closely to the warm, furry body of their mother. Cubs nurse at two- to three-hour intervals, with each nursing session lasting but a few minutes. At around 6 weeks of age the eyes of black bear cubs open. By this time they are mobile and have grown considerably, weighing four to seven pounds. Cubs born to larger females and those in smaller litters tend to receive more milk and grow the fastest. The milk of the black bear has a very high fat content (around 25 percent) compared to the milk of other mammal species, allowing cubs to easily quadruple their body weight in the space of a few weeks. Though not an appetizing topic for dinnertime conversation, it's worth noting that female black bears lick their tiny offspring to stimulate defecation. They then eat the feces, probably to keep the den clean. Maybe that's the real reason the sense of smell of sows remains dulled until they finish hibernation!

By the time they emerge from the den, the eyes of baby black bears have opened and their bodies are covered with fur. SHUTTERSTOCK

Nurturing Cubs to Adulthood

Black bear cubs are 2 to 3 months old when they emerge from the den with their mother. By this time they weigh eight pounds or more. Their ears look large in relation to the rest of their body, and the thin, gray fur they had at birth has thickened and become darker. While the mother is still somewhat lethargic in the days after exiting the den, and her digestive system needs some time to accept solid food, the cubs are full of energy. They run and play in the new outside world, but are watched carefully by their mother.

Cubs fresh from the den can rely on their mother's milk for nourishment, but it's a demanding time of the year for the sow. Perhaps that's part of the reason females with cubs are the last black bears to emerge from their dens. For a period of time the

Young black bear cubs are very energetic and playful. Shutterstock

mother will subsist primarily on leftovers from last year's food crop, or perhaps on the carrion of animals that died during the winter. Once the first shoots of green vegetation begin to emerge, the sow has more food options. Cubs begin testing solid foods and are eating them alongside their mother by midsummer, but will continue to nurse for about five months after emerging from the den.

Black bear cubs are very active, wrestling with one another, engaging in activities that appear to be impromptu games of tag or follow the leader. They also toy with objects. They're skilled tree climbers, a behavior that serves them well as youngsters.

Few predators pose a threat to black bear cubs protected by a vigilant mother. One of the most serious dangers cubs face is the male black bear, which sometimes kills cubs. Sows often tend their offspring near a "refuge tree," a large-trunked, tall tree that the cubs can climb. If danger threatens, the cubs scramble quickly up the refuge tree. In the case of a predatory black bear male, the larger animal is not likely to expend the effort needed to climb the tree in pursuit of the cubs. In the Great Lakes region, sows often choose broad, towering pines as refuge trees.

In late summer and fall, cubs undergo the same process of hyperphagia as adult bears. They voraciously consume all the food their mother discovers. If berry and nut crops are sparse and other food sources dwindle, this becomes a stressful and sometimes highly competitive period for sows with cubs. The sow must not only ingest enough forage to fatten herself, but must also produce milk for the cubs and find enough food to feed them as well.

Sows with cubs are among the first bears to den in the fall. The cubs hibernate with their mother (otherwise black bears rarely share a den). When the family surfaces the following spring, they'll stick together for a few months, until the mating season begins. Just prior to mating, the female will drive her young (now called yearlings) away. Yearling black bears usually wander away from the home range of their mother in a journey known as "dispersal," at which time they seek territories of their own.

Yearling black bears must learn to live on their own. Their success in finding a territory and managing their first solo hibernation are critical to long-term survival. SHUTTERSTOCK

Dispersing yearlings may become attracted to human sources of food, or may be struck by vehicles while crossing roads. They must find enough forage to fatten up for their first solo hibernation, and must avoid other dangers, including predation by large bears and, in some areas, wolf packs. If all goes well they'll secure a den and hibernate. When they emerge from hibernation as 2-year-olds, they've successfully transitioned to adult life.

CHAPTER 6 Black Bears and Other Animals

Black Bears and Other Predators

Black bears share their world with a variety of predators, depending on the part of the continent they occupy. These predators include carnivores as large as their grizzly bear cousins, which sometimes weigh more than 1,000 pounds, as well as sleek, petite weasels whose weight is measured in ounces. Black bears will gladly usurp the prey of smaller predators, but may also be the targets of predation under unusual circumstances.

The ranges of grizzly bears and black bears overlap across much of Alaska and northern Canada. National parks in southwestern Canada, such as Banff and Jasper National Parks, are also home to both creatures. In the contiguous United States, the tracks of both species dot the soil in Yellowstone and Grand Teton National Parks in Wyoming, Glacier National Park in Montana, and other wilderness locations in Wyoming, Montana, and Idaho. Almost without exception, black bears give grizzlies a wide berth. Grizzly bears are not only much larger, on average, than black bears; they are also more naturally aggressive, and far more likely to counter a perceived threat with an attack of their own. Large black bears may occasionally dominate smaller grizzlies when competing for food sources such as spawning fish or berries, but in most cases grizzly bears are the dominant bruin.

Predation of black bears by grizzlies is very rare, but has been documented. In Yellowstone National Park, researchers have found the carcass of a big black bear boar that had apparently been killed by a hulking male grizzly. The black bear's massive skull showed puncture wounds consistent with the crushing bite of a larger grizzly. Another Yellowstone incident involved the discovery of a dead black bear sow that was also presumably killed by a grizzly bear boar.

Black bears share their range with grizzlies in places like Yellowstone National Park, the home of this grizzly. Black bears generally give grizzlies a wide berth. SHUTTERSTOCK

However, in most situations, black bears can foil attempted predation by grizzlies. Avoiding a grizzly's space is their preferred means of dodging attacks, but if caught in close quarters, black bears will readily climb trees. Although young grizzlies can and do climb trees, and an adult grizzly may be able to reach 10 feet or more to pull a black bear from the branches, bear researchers believe grizzlies won't expend the energy needed to remove a "treed" black bear.

Wolf packs also constitute a threat to black bears, especially immature bears or sows with cubs, although aggressive interactions between the two species are rare. Again, a black bear's very best defense against a wolf pack attack is a speedy retreat up the nearest tree.

But even if caught in the open, a mature black bear can capably repel a small wolf pack if it stands its ground. However, under certain circumstances, wolves have been known to kill black bears and vice versa. Adult black bears have killed individual female wolves that were protecting the wolf's den site and pups. A study of the interactions between wolves and black bears in Minnesota over a ten-year period concluded that single wolves normally give way to black bears—even subadult black bears similar in size to the wolves. Incidents of wolves killing female and immature black bears have been recorded in the Canadian provinces of Ontario and Alberta.

Wolf packs sometimes pose a threat to black bears, and have killed denning bears, though these instances are certainly rare. SHUTTERSTOCK

Wolves sometimes prey upon denning black bears, with predation most likely successful on immature bears. However, in 1977 biologists recorded the killing of a 16-year-old sow and her cubs in northern Minnesota. The bear's den site consisted of a shallow depression under several midsize logs. In mid-February, a pack of wolves that had previously been observed as containing nine members attacked the bear from both sides of the den. The sow escaped the den, then fought the wolves as she fled some 25 yards to a large aspen tree. The wounded bear escaped up the tree, but later descended and returned to her den site, where she was either killed by the wolves or died from her wounds. Wolves were observed feeding on her carcass for some three weeks after the attack. Biologists speculate that a very light snowpack during the winter made the bear more vulnerable to predation. Additional snowpack would probably have made the bear's den much more difficult—or impossible—for the wolves to penetrate.

Hefty black bears dwarf even the largest mountain lions (cougars). On average, adult black bears are roughly twice as big as their cougar counterparts of the same sex. Nevertheless, mountain lions are fearsome predators capable of downing hoofed animals many times larger than themselves. Solitary, elusive creatures, mountain lions are seldom seen by humans in the wild. Recent studies have shed more light on the habits and behaviors of the mountain lion, but very little current evidence exists regarding interactions between black bears and cougars. Given their population densities and range, however, it is certain that the species frequently encounter one another.

A study of the interactions of mountain lions and bears in the northern Rocky Mountains documented numerous instances in which mountain lion kills of deer or elk were usurped by bears. Most of the bears chasing cougars from the carcasses were grizzlies. But black bears were also documented claiming mountain lion kills. A single instance of a mountain lion preying upon a black bear cub in Arizona has also been documented. A surprising number of historical accounts from the eighteenth and early nineteenth centuries tell of ferocious battles between

Black bears occasionally steal prey from mountain lions. Under very unusual circumstances, mountain lions may kill black bears. Shutterstock

mountain lions and bears (both black and grizzly). Most of these end with the death of the bear at the teeth and claws of the mountain lion, but several record the deaths of both combatants. As interesting as these accounts may be, current observations seem to indicate that, for the vast majority of time, black bears and mountain lions leave one another alone.

Black bears comingle with a host of smaller predators across their North American range. Lynx, bobcats, coyotes, and red foxes are found in black bear territories in a variety of regions.

These smaller predators might kill an orphan cub or challenge an immature black bear. They pose little threat to cubs protected by their mother. While it's quite likely that an adult black bear would displace these species from their prey if the opportunity arose, competition for food or other resources between black bears and these smaller predators is extremely rare.

Parasites and Diseases

Black bears are frequently bothered by a wide array of internal and external parasites. Their exposure to parasites depends upon the habitat and region of the continent they occupy, and is also somewhat determined by their diet. In Yellowstone National Park, for example, one research study concluded that grizzly bears had a much higher rate of infection by intestinal parasites than black bears. The researchers concluded the grizzlies were more often exposed to those parasites because their diet included a higher percentage of the carrion and prey animals that would host them.

Common internal parasites of black bears include round-worms and tapeworms. They may also be infected with parasites that live in other parts of the body, including the trichina worm. Some evidence indicates that black bears expel intestinal parasites just prior to hibernation, ridding themselves of organisms that could potentially drain energy reserves needed to survive the winter. Although high percentages of black bears in some areas host internal parasites, biologists have found little evidence that the infections typically become fatal or even cause significant health problems for the bruins. However, black bears are known to succumb to severe parasitic infections on occasion. University researchers investigating the death of a young bear in northern Idaho, which was thought to have succumbed to rabies, discovered the bear's brain, sinus tissues, and lungs were riddled with a tiny parasite from the fluke/flatworm family. The parasites were responsible for the rabieslike symptoms the bear exhibited shortly before its death.

In addition to internal parasites, black bears may be plagued with fleas, ticks, mosquitos, and biting flies. Ticks are common on

The long, dense coats of black bears protect them from many external parasites. Their ears and nose are most vulnerable to biting bugs. Shutterstock

bears but don't seem to cause any noticeable harm. Mosquitos have a difficult time reaching the skin of a black bear, but may attack exposed skin on its ears, nose, and face. Bears don't appear bothered by mosquitos and seldom exert much effort to rid themselves of the pests. They're much more aggressive toward biting flies. The bruins will swat incoming flies with their paws or snatch them with their teeth in lightning-quick bites.

North American black bears are remarkably free of diseases. The primary disease known to sometimes infect black bears is rabies. Several cases of rabid black bears have been recorded in a variety of places, but even this disease is quite rare.

Predation

The diet of the average black bears consists of more than 90 percent plant material. The remaining 10 percent, which is made up of animal protein, mostly comes from insects. Thus, the characteristic black bear is a casual carnivore at best.

However, those facts tend to minimize the black bear's potential as a predator. In some places, their predatory impact is notable. Certain animals, most possibly large, adept males, are much more predatory than the average bear. A study in central Idaho involving predation and elk calves is instructive. In an area with substantial populations of two large predators (black bears and mountain lions), 59 percent of all the elk calves researched in the study were killed by predators. Nearly 40 percent of the calves eliminated by predators were killed by black bears. Interestingly, black bear predation was highest on calves 5 weeks old and younger. Mountain lions also took many calves in the first month of life, but were far more effective than bears after the calves attained an age of 6 weeks.

Although the predation rates of black bears in this study are higher than those in studies conducted in other locations, the results demonstrate the predatory efficiency of black bears. Cow elk birth calves in identifiable, traditional "calving grounds" that are used year after year. It appears that individual black bears remember these enticing late-spring food sources and deliberately hunt newborn calves. Very young elk calves are nearly odorless and employ a hiding strategy to escape predation. By diligently searching calving areas and using their incredible senses of smell and eyesight, black bears are able to discover the secreted calves. Once discovered, the quick, agile bears can easily run down very young calves. Within weeks, however, elk calves become very fleet and can outrun all but the most persistent bears.

Moose, white-tailed deer, and mule deer do not gather at traditional birthing grounds like elk, making their young typically

Black bears are significant predators of young ungulates in some places. In the contiguous United States, they most often target elk calves and white-tailed deer fawns.

more dispersed and harder to find. Nonetheless, roaming black bears also prey upon deer fawns and moose calves in significant numbers in some places. Caribou calves may be similarly targeted by black bears in northern habitats.

Black bears occasionally prey upon adult ungulates, though these instances are rare. The animals they bring down are normally weakened by injury or malnutrition. Under such circumstances, a large black bear can kill deer, caribou, elk, or even moose.

Smaller prey is also taken by black bears. They dine on burrowing rodents with some frequency, although the methods of capturing them are different than those used by grizzly bears. Grizzlies often dig ground squirrels or other rodents from their burrows, using their massive claws as astonishingly efficient excavators. The claws of black bears are shorter and more sharply

Small rodents, such as this ground squirrel, are sometimes hunted by black bears.

curved than those of grizzlies, making them more useful for climbing trees than for digging. Thus, black bears tend to ambush rodents that have wandered from their dens. A research study of predation on yellow-bellied marmots in Colorado found that black bears killed fewer marmots than coyotes or badgers did, but more than hawks and eagles. Similar to elk calf predation, black bears probably have higher success preying upon rodents in the few weeks after young, inexperienced animals have emerged from their burrows in the spring.

The predatory instincts of black bears sometimes motivate them to attack livestock. Full-grown cattle or horses are at little risk of predation, but the bruins sometimes consume young calves.

Primarily plant eaters, black bears are very capable predators under the right circumstances. SHUTTERSTOCK

Black bears are more apt to prey upon sheep, and occasionally kill several sheep in a single predation event. Although the predation of livestock by black bears has little economic impact on the livestock industry on a nationwide scale, sheep farmers in some areas may lose a significant portion of their flock to bruins. A bear that repeatedly attacks livestock may be relocated or shot by wildlife officials.

Though the diet of a black bear consists primarily of plant matter, they're scientifically classified as carnivores. But perhaps the carnivore designation is helpful as a reminder that under the right circumstances, black bears are very capable predators.

CHAPTER 7 Black Bears and Humans

Black Bears in History

Long before the arrival of Europeans on the North American continent, indigenous peoples lived in proximity to black bears. Many American Indian tribes organized themselves into clans bearing the names of animals. For example, the Ojibwa (Chippewa) people in the Great Lakes region were originally organized into five clans named for various animals. Of these, the Bear Clan was by far the largest. The black bear (called "muckwa" in the native language) was sacred to the Ojibwa, but was also hunted and eaten by them.

Native peoples of the Pacific Northwest were aware of the Kermode bear, the creamy white color phase of the black bear, centuries before these unique bruins came to the attention of settlers. To the indigenous people the white bears, or "spirit bears," were sacred. One legend of indigenous origin recounts a bargain that was struck between Raven, the creator, and Black Bear. Raven wished for something to remind him of the primal age, when the land was covered in white glaciers and snowfields. After receiving Raven's word that he could lead a life of peace until the end of time, Black Bear consented to having one in ten of his people turn white. The white bears would serve as a reminder to Raven of the bygone era when the world was white and unhappy. For years, the native peoples did not speak of the Kermode bears to outsiders, a tradition that may have insulated this black bear population from European hunters.

American Indian hunters pursued black bears using a variety of methods. Bears were killed with the bow and arrow, but were also taken in deadfall traps. These consisted of a log that was supported by a stake with some type of bait attached. A bear that snatched the bait would topple the stake and be crushed under the log. Indigenous peoples in North America utilized the meat, hides, and fat of black bears. Bear hunts were often preceded

Black bears were both revered and hunted by American Indian tribes. Shutterstock

by ceremonial rituals, with another ceremony following the successful hunt. Many tribes viewed the black bear's hibernation as evidence of its potent spirit and mystical powers.

Settlement of the East Coast and the subsequent westward expansion of European immigration in the eighteen and nineteenth centuries spelled trouble for the black bear. As forests were converted to croplands and livestock brought onto farms on the edge of the wilderness, conflicts between bears and humans were inevitable. Black bears sometimes preyed upon livestock, and also took a liking to pioneers' vegetable gardens and crops. In New York state for example, almost 75 percent of the land was cleared for farming by 1900. Bears were killed as pests throughout the state, but were also diligently hunted for their hides, meat, and fat, which was rendered into bear grease.

Black bear hides were considered more valuable than those of grizzly bears, and for a time an active market for bear hides flourished in North America. In the 1700s thousands of black bear hides were exported to Europe. A bearskin was as valuable as a beaver pelt. The late 1700s and 1800s saw many states enact bounties (cash payments for dead animals) for black bears and other predators. Maine began offering a black bear bounty in 1770. Two counties in Maryland began offering bounties around 1750. Vermont's state legislature approved a $5 bounty on black bears in 1831. The bounty was increased to $15 in 1868, a handsome sum in an era when laborers might receive $1 as a day's wages. In New York state, a bounty was paid on black bears from 1892 to 1895.

Indiscriminate killing was one factor in the rapid decline of black bear populations across the contiguous United States in the nineteenth century, but habitat loss was a more acute problem. Wide-scale clearing of forests for agricultural purposes and timber eliminated mature nut-bearing trees in many locations,

The luxurious fur of black bears made their hides a value commodity for fur traders in the late 1700s. Shutterstock

The catastrophic destruction of the American chestnut tree (fruit shown here) in the eastern United States deprived black bears of an important source of food. Sᴴᴜᴛᴛᴇʀsᴛᴏᴄᴋ

and deprived the bruins of the forested haunts in which they're most at home. Further compounding habitat loss in the East was the near-complete destruction of the American chestnut tree, which took place from the 1920s to the 1940s. American chestnut blight, a disease caused by a fungus, killed most of the chestnut trees in the United States, depriving black bears and other wildlife species of one of the most bountiful nut crops of eastern forests.

Black Bears in Modern Times

Several "modern" movements in American culture contributed to a broad recovery of black bear population, some beginning as early as the late 1800s. In 1885, New York state created the Catskill and Adirondack Forest Preserves, which later became Catskill Park and Adirondack Park. The preservation of wilderness habitat in these areas buffered black bears from further habitat loss. In the same time period, the federal government began creating national parks. In the West, Yellowstone and Yosemite were designated national parks prior to 1900, preserving critical habitat for black bears and other species. Shenandoah National Park and Great Smoky Mountains National Park were created in 1926 and 1934 respectively, providing black bears important refuges in the East.

However, cultural and economic trends during the same time period were also instrumental in renewing black bear populations across much of their range. Industrialization brought human populations to the cities. Much of the land enthusiastically deforested for farm fields was found to be too rocky or not sufficiently fertile to profitably grow crops. Marginal farmlands were abandoned across much of the East from 1900 to 1950. The land reverted to forest, increasing habitat for black bears.

The creation of hunting seasons and the protection of black bears as a game animal were also important to the species' recovery in the United States. Unregulated bear hunting ceased in New York state in 1903, when black bears were given status as a game animal and protected from being hunted in July and August. A more structured hunting season and bag limits were established in 1923, the same year Montana designated black

Parks and wildlife refuges provide black bears with protected habitat and have been instrumental in their recovery. This bear was photographed at the Alligator River National Wildlife Refuge in North Carolina. USFWS/STEVE HILLEBRAND

bears a game species. Michigan gave black bears protection as a game animal and instituted a hunting season in 1925. By the 1950s, black bears were protected by hunting laws that strictly regulated harvest rates and hunting season dates throughout most of the United States.

It is largely accepted among biologists that black bear populations in North America reached their lows sometime around 1950, or perhaps a decade or two before. Since then, *Ursus americanus* has staged a remarkable comeback, both in numbers and distribution. State wildlife agencies often classify the status of animal species as "declining," "stable," or "increasing" in relation to population. In the vast majority of locations where their numbers and range are recorded, black bears are classified as "stable" or "increasing." The growth of black bear populations and range in some areas is quite dramatic. The number of square miles of habitat occupied in North Carolina by black bears showed a seven-fold increase from 1971 to 2010. Bears are believed to inhabit more habitat in North Carolina at the present time than they have for 150 years. Even in southern states, where bears were eradicated and have been classified as endangered or threatened species, populations appear to be thriving. In Georgia, for instance, black bears were nearly eliminated in the 1930s. Currently, some 5,100 bears roam the state in three population areas.

Limitations to black bear range expansion are primarily related to small, fragmented portions of habitat where bears are poorly buffered from human disturbance and dangers posed by human activity. Roads, for example, can be perilous to black bears. Death caused by collisions with vehicles is a significant factor in bear mortality in some places. Researchers have found that boars are more often killed by vehicles than sows. Young males dispersing into new territory in the spring appear particularly vulnerable to roadkill. However, biologists have also determined mortality from vehicle collisions also claims a noteworthy number of females, particularly in southern states. Both sexes are at higher risk on roads during the late summer and autumn, when they cover more territory in search of food.

Roads represent a peril for black bears. Collisions with vehicles are a significant source of bear mortality in some areas. SHUTTERSTOCK

Humans and Black Bears: Current Interactions and Precautions

Black bears have no natural predators in most areas of North America. They are also notably resistant to disease and are seldom harmed by parasites. Although their reproduction rates are quite low compared to other large animals, such as white-tailed deer, these factors allow populations to persist and thrive wherever they find suitable habitat.

At the present time, humans are the dominant source of black bear mortality in the contiguous United States. They are killed both deliberately and indirectly by humans. Hunting is the number one source of human-caused mortality. The International Union for Conservation of Nature (IUCN) estimates that 40,000 to 50,000 black bears are harvested annually by hunters in the United States and Canada. The majority of biologists agree that carefully regulated hunting poses little or no threat to black bear populations. Boars are taken more regularly by hunters than sows, which reduces the reproductive impacts of hunting. Collisions with vehicles and lethal removal of "problem" bears are the other primary sources of human-caused mortality to black bears, though those impacts are much smaller than hunting.

Given their omnivorous eating habits, it should come as no surprise that black bears will happily eat human and pet food. In the days of open, unfenced garbage dumps, black bears were frequent visitors to refuse heaps, scrounging through the rubble for vegetable peelings, bread crusts, rotting meat scraps, and whatever other morsels might attract their attention. The 1950s and 1960s saw a curious tourist industry develop in relation to the bears (black and grizzly) in Yellowstone National Park. Motorists fed begging bears along the roadsides, with the freeloading bruins sometimes crawling into automobiles and trashing the interiors in search of more grub.

Although the deliberate feeding of bears is now illegal in state and national parks, visitors sometimes unwittingly create "nuisance" or "problem" bears that actively seek human

Black bears were treated as novelties—almost pets—in Yellowstone National Park prior to the 1960s. Here, in an undated photo, President Calvin Coolidge strolls past begging black bears on a visit to Yellowstone. YELLOWSTONE NATIONAL PARK

food. Unattended food baskets and coolers may be raided by black bears at picnic areas. Campers who fail to store food beyond the reach of bears sometimes discover their larders consumed by bruins. People cooking in the outdoors who leave behind scraps and crumbs also create a potential association between humans and food in the consciousness of bears. Additionally, bears will gladly gobble dog food and other pet foods, especially during periods of hyperphagia. In many areas, the most common complaint received from wildlife officials regarding black bears is their destruction of bird feeders and consumption of birdseed.

Black Bears

Bears that frequent human habitation in search of food are a difficult problem for wildlife managers. In early times, nuisance bears were often trapped and relocated to remote areas with proper habitat. However, bears have an uncanny homing instinct. Research studies from a number of areas demonstrate that about 50 percent of relocated black bears return to their homes within a few days, traveling distances up to 40 miles. Relocation also potentially puts the transported bear into competition with local bruins. When relocation is ineffective and a bear continually invades human habitation in search of food, wildlife managers often have little choice but to lethally remove the bear.

A bear that learns to associate humans with food may take up residence around homes and cabins. This situation is never beneficial to the bear. Shutterstock

Keeping black bears from exploiting human food sources is usually as simple as removing the attractant. This includes utilizing "bear-proof" trash containers and dumpsters in rural areas, cleaning up after cooking outdoors, and storing food out of the reach of bears when camping.

Despite these precautions, people may still encounter black bears when recreating outdoors. Some folks worry that such experiences may be dangerous, that black bears may maul or kill them. While a handful of humans have been killed by black bears in the past century, lightning strikes and attacks by domestic dogs have claimed far more lives than black bears. Members of

Increasing numbers of black bears in the United States in the past few decades have improved wildlife watchers' odds of sighting one of these fascinating animals. Shutterstock

UNEASY ICONS?

Black bears played a starring role in the myths and legends of many ancient peoples. They've also captured iconic roles in popular culture. The inspiration for the name "Winnie" in A. A. Milne's classic work of children's literature, *Winnie-the-Pooh,* traces directly to a black bear. During World War I, a Canadian officer purchased a black bear cub from a Canadian hunter while on his way to England. He snuck the cub into England and named it "Winnie" in honor of Winnipeg, Manitoba. The cub was eventually housed at the London Zoo, where it was seen by Christopher, the son of A. A. Milne. Christopher named his toy bear Winnie, from whence his father took the name for his fictional bear, Winnie-the-Pooh.

Popular as children's toys, the "teddy bear" is named for President Theodore "Teddy" Roosevelt. In 1902, Roosevelt was invited on a bear hunt by the governor of Mississippi. After a few days of hunting, during which the president failed to take a bruin, the party's hunting guide had the opportunity to corner and capture a black bear, which he tied to a tree. Roosevelt was summoned to shoot the bear, but he refused. The outing was well covered by the press, and a political cartoon showing the president disdainfully shunning the guide and the tied bear appeared in the *Washington Post* shortly after the incident. Although the actual bear was an adult, subsequent cartoon characterizations of the event showed a smaller, cuter bear with the appearance of a cub. A toy shop owner saw the cartoons and was inspired to create a stuffed toy bear, which he marketed as "Teddy's bear." The creations became an immediate success and have been staples of the American toy market ever since.

Concerned that forest fires could wipe out needed timber resources during World War II, the US Forest Service and War Advertising Council worked diligently to reach the American public with a message of fire prevention. In 1944 they jointly created an advertising campaign using a forest animal, a bear, as the fire prevention mascot. Thus began the fictional career of "Smokey Bear," named for a heroic former assistant chief of the New York City Fire Department. In 1950, a black bear cub was found by firefighters working to extinguish a catastrophic forest fire in New Mexico. The cub's burns were treated, and it became the living representation of Smokey Bear, finding a new home in the National Zoo in Washington DC. For decades, advertising and cartoon representations of Smokey Bear have encouraged the prevention and extinction of forest fires on public lands.

Ironically, the past couple of decades have found more and more biologists questioning a policy of across-the-board suppression of forest fires. Prior to human intervention, forest fires were part of a natural process of forest regeneration that benefitted numerous wildlife species, including black bears. Do we still need Smokey? To the extent he encourages people to be careful with fire, he's certainly been beneficial. But biologists who manage wildlife habitat on forested public lands might now argue that Smokey's portrayal of forest fires as bad was actually counterproductive to many wild animals, including his own species.

the *Ursus americanus* species are generally shy of humans. When confronted at close range, black bears may huff and stomp the ground with their forepaws. However, these behaviors are more an indication of the bear's discomfort than the prelude to an aggressive attack.

In the rare cases when black bears do attack people, their intentions are most often predatory. Experts advise recreationists to "play dead" if rushed by a grizzly bear. A black bear attack should be handled in the opposite manner. Biologists encourage people to fight back, punching, kicking, and yelling at the bear. Blows to the bruin's sensitive nose may be particularly effective in repelling an attack. The idea is to present the bear with a formidable foe versus an easy meal.

The largest carnivore in the region, a black bear sighting at an eastern state or national park is a thrilling experience for most visitors. Bruin behavior is fascinating to observe, and the animal's presence is a compelling reminder that its species' history and future are an important part of our own.

Index

About the Author

A writer, photographer, and naturalist, Jack Ballard is a frequent contributor to numerous regional and national publications. He has written hundreds of articles on wildlife and wildlife-related topics.

His photos have been published in numerous books (Smithsonian Press, Heinemann Library, etc.), calendars, and magazines. Jack has received multiple awards for his writing and photography from the Outdoor Writers Association of America and other professional organizations. He holds two master's degrees and is an accomplished public speaker, entertaining students, conference attendees, and recreation/conservation groups with his compelling narratives. When not wandering the backcountry, he hangs his hat in Red Lodge, Montana. See more of his work at jackballard.com.